GALAXY OF SUPERSTARS

CHELSEA HOUSE PUBLISHERS

Want strong bones? Your bones grow until about age 35 and the calcium in milk helps. After that, it helps keep them strong. Chicks rule.

got milk?

GALAXY OF SUPERSTARS

Dixie Chicks

Concetta Seminara-Kennedy

CHELSEA HOUSE PUBLISHERS
Philadelphia

Frontis: The Dixie Chicks appeared in their own "Got Milk?" ad, showing that their popularity has truly crossed over into the mainstream.

CHELSEA HOUSE PUBLISHERS
Editor in Chief: Sally Cheney
Director of Production: Kim Shinners
Creative Manager: Takeshi Takahashi
Manufacturing Manager: Diann Grasse

Staff for DIXIE CHICKS
Associate Editor: Ben Kim
Picture Researcher: Jane Sanders
Production Assistant. Jaimie Winkler
Series Designer: Takeshi Takahashi
Cover Designer: Terry Mallon
Layout: 21st Century Publishing and Communications, Inc.

The Chelsea House World Wide Web address is
http://www.chelseahouse.com

First Printing

1 3 5 7 9 8 6 4 2

Library of Congress Cataloging-in-Publication Data

Seminara-Kennedy, Concetta.
    The Dixie Chicks / Concetta Seminara-Kennedy.
        p. cm. — (Galaxy of superstars)
Summary: Chronicles the rise to fame of the girl group whose music
combines the traditional sounds of country with a mixture of modern
country, Texas swing, bluegrass, and a touch of rockabilly.
Includes bibliographical references (p.   ).
    ISBN 0-7910-6768-8
    1. Dixie Chicks (Musical group)—Juvenile literature. 2. Country musicians
—United States—Biography—Juvenile literature. [1. Dixie Chicks (Musical
group) 2. Musicians. 3. Country music. 4. Women—Biography.] I. Title.
II. Series.
ML3930.D58 S46 2002
781.642'092'2—dc21

                                                            2002000603

CONTENTS

FROM HONKY TONKS
TO CENTER STAGE

The Dixie Chicks—Martie Seidel, Emily Robison, and Natalie Maines—practically floated up to the stage to accept their first Country Music Award. Their presence at the annual ceremony, held at the Grand Ole Opry in Nashville, Tennessee on September 23, 1998, was the result of nine years of dedication to performing at honky tonks, restaurants, and private functions all over the world.

First the Dixie Chicks accepted the Horizon Award, which is bestowed on the best new promising performer or group. Their competitors for this honor were Trace Adkins, Jo Dee Messina, Michael Peterson, and Lee Ann Womak. Emily Erwin, who plays banjo, dobro (an acoustic guitar with steel resonating discs inside the body under the bridge), guitar, and acoustic bass, thanked God at this exciting moment in her career, saying "I have been so blessed."

But the magic of the night was far from over. The Dixie Chicks had also been nominated for Group of the Year. They never thought they could win the award because the members of the Dallas trio were relative newcomers to the Nashville country music scene. Other nominees for Group of the Year included Alabama, Diamond Rio, The Mavericks, and Sawyer Brown. Imagine how stunned the Dixie Chicks

---

The Dixie Chicks burst onto the country scene and have since taken it by storm with their crossover appeal—both in their music and in their glamorous fashion style.

were to be called once again to center stage for their second award of the evening. The usually quiet Emily exclaimed, "My heart stopped beating when they called our name!"

Only one year earlier, at the 1997 Country Music Awards, the Dixie Chicks were seated in the balcony. They were surrounded by other loyal fans of country music and could barely see the stage. They never thought that they would be accepting not one, but two, Country Music Awards just 12 months later. At the 1998 ceremony the Dixie Chicks had reserved seats in the front of the auditorium near country music superstars Shania Twain and Garth Brooks.

On that September evening, Martie, the band's violinist (or "fiddler") held back her tears and said, "Thanks for letting us color outside the lines." Indeed, the members of the Dixie Chicks had always followed this independent and individualistic philosophy since the band's original members had joined together in 1989 to make bluegrass music. (This type of music is played on unamplified stringed instruments and often involves improvisation.)

It was in 1989 that sisters Emily and Martie Erwin met Laura Lynch and Robin Macy to form the bluegrass quartet. Laura Lynch was a former stockbroker and corporate real estate agent who sang and played bass guitar in the group. She remained in the group until 1995. Her main function in the early years was working on the group's marketing strategies. Robin Macy was the band's original lead singer and played acoustic guitar. During the band's earlier years, she was a math teacher at St. Mark's School for Boys. In 1992 when the Dixie Chicks were in the process of changing their musical sound to a more modern one, Robin decided to move onto another more traditional bluegrass group called the Domestic Science Club. Natalie Maines, the newest member and present lead singer of the Dixie Chicks, would join the group in 1995 when she was attending Texas Tech University. She is responsible for much of the current sound and look of the band.

The Dixie Chicks' first step toward fame took place on the busy street corners of Dallas's West End, where the girls played for tips. They made $300 during their first hour of street performance. Sometimes literally hundreds of people would gather to hear the girls play well-known country songs and their original material. When their outdoor audience members would ask for their band name, the girls were embarrassed to admit they didn't have one. One day on their way to a street performance, they heard the 1973 Little Feat song "Dixie Chicken" on the radio and decided to name themselves the Dixie Chickens. Eventually, this original name became the "Dixie Chicks."

Before the Chicks were being hailed for their outstanding talent and voices, they were performing at such low-key venues as state fairs and Joey Tomato's restaurant in Dallas. The group prided itself on never refusing to perform at any type of party or function. They were an inexpensive *and* talented group to hire. From birthday parties for local celebrities to funerals, they played them all. All the while they kept their dream of striking a big record contract with one of the record companies on Nashville's Music Row.

The group's first form of transportation in the Dallas area was Emily's gray Caprice Classic—a far-from-glamorous vehicle. Later the band could afford a van for their tours around the country. They eventually moved into a pink motor home before nationwide fame struck. During their tours, the Dixie Chicks stayed in some unappealing hotels. Natalie recalls of her early touring days with the band, "Even when we got our own rooms we were still in sleazy motels."

The Dixie Chicks' particular brand of country music combines the traditional sounds of country with a mixture of modern country, Texas swing, bluegrass, and a touch of rockabilly. The Dixie Chicks strive to embody the spirit of empowered females living out their dreams and ambitions in today's world, be it in the recording studio or in corporate meeting rooms. The name of their band was criticized for being demeaning to women, but the group's perseverance and musical talent have quickly silenced those critics. It didn't take long for fans of the Dixie Chicks and their uplifting message of "Chick Power" to spread throughout the United States and the world.

In 1998 the group released its first album, *Wide Open Spaces*, with its new label, Monument Records, and had its first hit with "I Can Love You Better." Sales of the album increased for eight weeks in a row. The album became a certified gold record faster than any other album in the Sony Nashville sales history. The women were the best-selling country group and top debut performers of the year. In that year, no other debut country album had as many hits (three to be exact). National publications such as *Rolling Stone* and *Harper's Bazaar* praised them, not only for their ability to stand out among new and old country groups, but also for their ability to bring a fresh new vibe to the country music world. It seemed like things just couldn't get any better—but then the Country Music Awards proved that there was still more in store for the Chicks.

On that award-filled September evening in 1998, the Chicks wore conservative evening dresses—not the kind of outfits that usually mark their stage performances. Their look can be described as glamorous and cutting-edge. It has sparked its share of controversy among country music's straight-laced critics. In fact, Natalie, the vocalist and most outspoken member of the group, proposed that the members each have small chick feet tattooed on the tops of their feet to mark each gold record and number one hit that the band earns. In true Dixie Chick style, Emily and Martie agreed. Since their first hit with "Wide Open Spaces," their feet have been covered with 10 other tiny tattoos!

But back in 1989, the Dixie Chicks' look and classic bluegrass sound reflected a time when a nice (cow)girl wore the traditional cowboy hat, ornately-fringed blouses with matching skirts—and cowboy boots, of course.

Sheryl Crow with the Dixie Chicks. Their unique take on country music has attracted a wide audience as well as fellow musicians.

2

TWO CHICKS
HATCH AND GROW

Martha Eleanor Erwin was born on October 12, 1969, in York, Pennsylvania, thousands of miles away from Dallas, Texas. Her parents, Barbara and Paul were both schoolteachers. Martie also had an older sister, Julia. On August 16, 1972, a third daughter, Emily, was born to the family in their new home of Pittsfield, Massachusetts. Shortly after Emily's birth, the Erwins decided to move to the warmer climate of Texas. They had been offered teaching positions at Greenhill High School, a private school located in an exclusive community in the Dallas-Fort Worth area.

After the Erwins moved to Texas, they insisted that their daughters attend symphony concerts with them. Paul Erwin was the first to take his children to bluegrass and country music festivals and concerts. Both parents wanted the girls to acquire musical appreciation at a young age. While in elementary school, Martie and Emily began to take violin lessons. The girls were taught by the Suzuki method, which stresses repetition. Their mother made sure they practiced each day and kept an egg timer nearby to track how long they practiced. Little did the girls know that their mother's dedication to their musical education would have such an

Dallas, Texas, where the Erwin sisters grew up and started playing music. Although Texas is well-known for its affinity for country music, their father Paul took them to see symphony concerts as well as bluegrass and country music festivals.

incredible result in their adult lives. In one of their first performances, the girls were enlisted by their mother to play at the family's garage sale.

Martie and Emily attended Greenhill High School. They both played on the girls' soccer team and in the school orchestra (earning them the nickname "Orch Dorks," according to Emily) and had active social lives. But the majority of their spare time went to practicing their musical instruments. While both girls began their musical education with violin lessons, Emily eventually decided to specialize in the banjo as well as the mandolin and dobro. By the time she was 12, Emily had already made her stage debut as the opening act for country music star Ricky Skaggs. Meanwhile, Martie went from studying the classical violin to country fiddle with ease. Her violin teacher, Johnny Thorn, taught Martie between the ages of 11 and 16. Though Thorn never imagined one of his pupils would someday be a country music star, he knew that Martie had talent. She was competing in national fiddle contests and winning frequently.

One of the key ingredients to the success of the Dixie Chicks is the sisterly bond of Emily and Martie. This family connection can be heard in the way in which they harmonize their voices, as well as in the way they play their respective instruments together. From the quality of their musicianship, it's obvious that the girls have been playing together since they were children. Emily herself happily admits, "Playing together is all I've ever known."

Martie's musical influences include Tim O'Brien, Mark O'Connor, Eddy Stubbs, Sam Bush, Joe Venuti, and Alison Krauss. Among her musical influences, Emily counts Bela Fleck, Emmylou Harris, Glen Campbell, Jerry Douglas,

Dolly Parton, and Shawn Colvin. But the sisters' biggest inspiration to succeed in the music industry started at home with their parents, who drove them to and attended competitions, lessons, and practices throughout the girls' elementary and high school years. Emily is thankful for her parents, whom she refers to as "the one unconditional constant" in her life.

From 1984 to 1987, Emily and Martie played in the Blue Night Express, a bluegrass group made up of four teenagers. The other two members of the group were brother and sister Troy and Sharon Gilchrist. It gave them their first taste of being in a musical group and working as a team with other like-minded musicians. Emily still recalls her humble beginnings: "Martie got to join when she was twelve, and when I got to be twelve I joined." The girls were not afraid that their taste in bluegrass would differ from that of their peers, who might enjoy rock or more contemporary country music. They stuck to their musical ambitions without trying to follow the "in crowd." With Blue Night Express, they had the opportunity to tour the state of Texas and out-of-state music festivals. In their late teens, the girls already were professional musicians with experience under their belts.

After Martie graduated from Greenhill High School in 1987, she attended Georgetown College for a year. In 1988 she received a scholarship and transferred to Southern Methodist University (SMU) where she was a music theory major. When she wasn't studying at SMU, she spent her free time playing shows with the newly-formed Dixie Chicks. Balancing her time between a demanding academic schedule and a band that gave 100 percent to every performance was tiring for the young coed. During this hectic time,

Joe Venuti was a jazz violinist who was also one of Martie's influences.

Martie told Liz Gordon at the *Dallas Morning News*: "My friends think I have it all—school and the band. . . . I study as much as they do. I just play with the band instead of watching television." At one point in 1991 after that interview, Martie decided she had to choose between her education and life on the road with the Dixie Chicks. The band won.

During high school, Emily had dreamed of joining the United States Air Force and becoming a jet pilot. She was lucky to have very understanding teachers who would let her make up work when she was involved in musical competitions or performing with Blue Night Express, and later with the Dixie Chicks. She never forgot their patience and understanding of her devotion to music. Emily was even voted president of her senior class. But her love of music won over her yearning to conquer the blue skies or apply for college.

Not everything in the lives of Martie and Emily was happy and exciting. In 1989, Paul and Barbara Erwin decided that their marriage must come to an end. Divorce is never easy for any family to endure, but Emily and Martie survived the trials of their parents' divorce. They remain very close to their parents, who have both remarried. The song "You Were Mine," which appears on the *Wide Open Spaces* album was inspired by the events surrounding the divorce of their parents:

> I took out all the pictures of our wedding day
> It was a time of love and laughter
> Happy ever after
> But even those old pictures have begun to fade

Even in their time of emotional trial, the parents who had given so much to their daughters inspired them musically.

THE DIXIE CHICKS UNITE

The four original members of the Dixie Chicks met in 1989. Laura Lynch and Robin Macy had seen the Erwin sisters perform with Blue Night Express. As the girls were approaching summer vacation and the prospect of working at the mall like many of their peers, Laura and Robin approached the Erwins about forming a new band. Robin had already worked in musical theater. She was drawn to the Erwin sisters' combination of youth, charm, and serious talent. She said of her commitment to the band, "We're following a dream." Laura also could not resist the opportunity to join the talented sister duo. She referred to being in the Dixie Chicks as a "miracle." Though there was roughly a 12-year age gap between the Erwin sisters and Laura and Robin, it was hardly noticeable, and the group initially worked well as a band. Martie and Emily were mature and professional despite their young ages.

Laura took it upon herself to be the group's unofficial marketing representative. She even devised the 'chick' logo— a round chick with long eyelashes. Laura said, "Marketing that band was the only thing I thought of. When I woke up in the morning, I thought about how I could market the band."

Martie playing her violin. By the time the first incarnation of the Dixie Chicks got together in 1989, Martie and Emily were already seasoned veterans, having played with Blue Night Express.

One of the first ways the group drew attention to itself was by sending out a newsletter entitled *Chick Chat* to fans who signed onto a mailing list that was available at Dixie Chick performances. In the newsletter you could find their latest tour news, silly anecdotes, the group members' opinions on a wide range of unrelated topics (such as the places with the best diner food), and colorful quotes. You could also purchase tapes, records, T-shirts, and even coloring books.

In a matter of months, the group went from street corner performers to performing in restaurants and bars and on to playing private parties. It was not at all glamorous, but it was paid work nonetheless. Eventually, both Robin and Laura left their day jobs. The private parties they played progressed from middle-class get-togethers to extravagant parties hosted by billionaire Ross Perot and United States Senator John Tower. The senator's daughter, Penny Cook, enjoyed their music so much that she loaned them the funds necessary for their studio recording sessions.

The Dixie Chicks could now be found in the recording studio. Though they were not yet signed to a major record label, they produced three records independently. (The type of records they made are known as "indie" records.) It was important to them that they establish a distinct recorded 'sound' that their listening audience could easily identify. The Dixie Chicks released their first recording in 1991, a Christmas single entitled "Home on the Radar Range" produced by Larry Seyer. With their first album, *Thank Heavens for Dale Evans*, released in 1992, the Chicks paid tribute to the country recording and film star of the 1930s and 1940s. Dale Evans was not only famous for being married to Roy Rogers, but

Roy Rogers and Dale Evans, the namesake for the Dixie Chicks' 1992 album *Thank Heavens for Dale Evans*.

she was also known as an independent woman. The Chicks even included her image on the album cover alongside their own photographs, and were even dressed in the traditional cowgirl look to match their idol. The songs they presented on this album included "I Want to be a Cowboy's Sweetheart," which was written in 1932 by Patsy Montana but updated by the Chicks for a 1990s audience.

During the recording of their next album, *Little Ol' Cowgirl*, released in 1992, Robin was stressed. She felt great pressure to sing her best and even cried at the recording sessions. The Chicks' second indie recording effort, though overlooked by the Nashville recording industry, contained a diverse array of songs. There was an "Irish Medley," as well as a spiritual song, "Hallelujah, I Just Love Him So" that had previously been performed by R&B star Ray Charles. The variety on that album points to the identity problems that were tearing the group apart: Should they follow the bluegrass path? Or should they adopt a more widely-acccptcd country sound?

By the time the Chicks had recorded *Little Ol' Cowgirl*, there was already tension surrounding the musical direction of the band. In 1992 Robin decided to leave the band because she was seeking a different musical path from the rest of the band members. The Chicks third and final indie country album, *Shouldn't a Told You That*, was released in 1993. On this record, both band members and the band's musicians contributed to writing songs like "I'm Falling Again" and "One Heart Away." This album also contains the only recording of Martie singing lead vocal on "I Wasn't Looking for You."

The group always hoped that a major record company recruiter would discover them at one of their shows. They wanted the chance to add their names to the history of American country music. Laura told *Billboard* magazine, "Record labels want something we're not. We think we're about to hit a happy medium [with *Shouldn't a Told You That*]." Laura had enlisted the help of Buddy Lee Attractions, a booking agency that arranged all of the group's performances. Through their connection at the agency, they met David Skepner, who became their manager and would work with them until 1999. David had already forged a respected career managing country superstar Loretta Lynn.

However, the man who made it his job to get the Chicks the early recognition they were working toward so passionately was Simon Renshaw, a man the Chicks described as "cocky." It was Simon who introduced the women to Blake Chancey, a vice president at Sony Records who planned to produce their first album. Finally, the recording dream they had been striving toward for years seemed to be coming true.

Meanwhile, the instrumental elements of the group had begun to change as early as 1991. The Chicks hired a drummer, Tom Van Schaik, in their effort to be less traditional and more contemporary sounding. (Robin had strongly disagreed with the decision to hire a drummer.) After Robin's departure, the Chicks hired a new guitarist to take her place. One significant temporary addition to the band occurred during the recording of *Little Ol' Cowgirl*. Lloyd Maines was hired to play steel guitar on the album. He was a renowned steel guitarist who had played in the Maines Brothers Band since the late 1970s and had a respected reputation as a studio musician. The Chicks decided to ask Lloyd to stay on and play at several of their shows. If Lloyd's last name sounds familiar, it's because he is the father of the Natalie, the present lead singer of the Dixie Chicks. At the time Lloyd was playing on *Little Ol' Cowgirl*, Natalie was still in high school being a cheerleader and singing in her school's performance group.

The road kept calling the Dixie Chicks. It was partly due to their tireless effort to stay on the road and spread their vibrant brand of music that ultimately helped them to succeed. In 1991 they played for President and Mrs. George Bush Sr. at the Kennedy Center in Washington at the Texas Heritage Festival. They also headed to New York City on an Amtrak train. The Chicks were determined to make an impromptu appearance on *The Late Show with David Letterman*, a talk show known for its wacky, off-the-cuff type of humor. Unfortunately, the Chicks didn't know that playing in the lobby of the NBC Building did *not* ensure that you would be asked to perform on the show. Instead, they were escorted out of the lobby by a security guard—just another day in New York City!

The group did manage to raise enough cash playing on the streets of Manhattan to afford a posh hotel room for themselves and the band. They had a few other interesting opportunities to gain national exposure in 1991 as well. Their rendition of "I Want to Be a Cowboy's Sweetheart" from *Thank Heavens for Dale Evans* was used in an episode of the once-popular television program *Northern Exposure*. They also sang the jingle in a McDonald's commercial heard by millions.

Taking their show across the Atlantic Ocean was an exciting moment for the Dixie Chicks. They played in Europe for the first time in 1992 and performed at a country music festival in Zurich, Switzerland. Laura recalled, "We got our rhinestone garb on and met the mayor, and he gave us an official invitation to the city." The group also played in Monaco and at a famous jazz bar in Paris, which was not their usual environment. They had gigs at the Texas-style saloon at Eurodisney (located outside of Paris) and at Thunderbirds, the only Mexican restaurant in Brussels, Belgium. Now the Dixie Chicks had an expanded audience that included Europe, and their new fans' smiles and applause needed no translation for the band.

Perhaps the crowning moment of the their early years was a performance at the Tennessee Inaugural Ball of President William Jefferson

Clinton at the Washington Hilton held on January 20, 1993. The Dixie Chicks wrote about the experience in their newsletter: "Various elegant folks were whispering, 'They must be from Dallas.' I think it was the hair which we poofed up bigger'n trash can lids!" Johnny Cash, another country performer whom the girls had always admired, was also at the ball.

A president from Arkansas known for his musical abilities knew exactly who should be playing at one of the most important parties of his life.

4

A NEW CHICK
CHANGES EVERYTHING

Lloyd Maines and his wife Tina brought Natalie into the world on October 14, 1974, in Lubbock, Texas. Natalie Louise Maines was born into a family of the country music elite. Lloyd Maines had released albums with the Maines Brothers Band from 1978 to 1991. The group even had a Top 25 hit with "Everybody Needs Love on a Saturday Night." He was an outstanding studio musician who had played on albums by the Joe Ely Band, Guy Clark, Uncle Tupelo, and others. The Dixie Chicks recruited his steel guitar talents for the *Little Ol' Cowgirl* album. He was also hired to play with the Chicks during their live opening act. Lloyd first worked with the Dixie Chicks in 1991, while Natalie was still in high school. Natalie could not help but gather a genuine appreciation for country music: "Country music was so prevalent in our family that I was fortunate to be exposed to it at a very early age."

Natalie always had a penchant for the dramatic. When she was in the second grade, the precocious tot announced to her teacher she didn't need to learn math because she was going to be a star. At Lubbock High School she was a definite extrovert, finding her place performing as a cheerleader as a freshman and in the school's performance singing group "Western

Natalie Maines joined the Dixie Chicks in 1995 and immediately had an impact on the group—not only on their sound but in their look and attitude.

Union." Natalie's musical tastes were geared more toward the pop and folk sounds of James Taylor, the Indigo Girls, and Bonnie Raitt than the country music of Kenny Rogers or Reba McIntyre. (Natalie also has a special affection for John Travolta, who is more famous for his acting talents than for his pop albums released during the 1970s.)

For Natalie, who is petite at 5 ft. 3 in., weight has always been a sensitive issue. Our society is especially critical of entertainers who aren't stick-thin. But Natalie, whose weight has fallen and risen throughout her time in the Dixie Chicks, focuses on both her inner beauty and her exterior look.

Natalie began her pursuit of a college education at West Texas A&M, where she was deciding on a major. Her first course selections were geared toward a career in radio broadcasting. Natalie was definitely enjoying the social aspects of the college experience—perhaps a little too much. The following year she transferred to South Plains College, which was close to her parents' home in Lubbock. Her father was on the advisory committee of the school and also taught classes there. It was during her studies at South Plains that she met and fell in love with her future husband, Michael Tarabay. The couple wed on May 9, 1997.

Natalie began to focus on her singing abilities. She was accepted to the Berklee School of Music in Boston, Massachusetts, and received a scholarship to study singing. She chose to pursue the diploma program at this well-known music school. She stayed for the spring 1995 semester until she felt the call to return home. Before joining the Dixie Chicks, Natalie was again in Texas, attending Texas Tech University for the summer session. It was clear that this young lady could not seem to find her own niche in an institution of higher learning.

While Natalie was sorting out her academic

life, the Dixie Chicks finally achieved their dream of striking a contract with Sony thanks to Simon Renshaw's contacts. Like any proud father, Lloyd Maines suggested his baby girl when the Erwin sisters were looking for a new vocalist to transform the sound of their group. He had given Emily and Martie copies of the demonstration tape Natalie used in her audition for the Berklee School. The Erwin sisters listened to it and were so impressed that they both blurted out Natalie's name when suggesting a new lead singer to each other. Both had been driving around Dallas with the cassette in their respective cars mulling it over at stop signs and red lights.

Natalie had an unofficial audition for the Dixie Chicks. The Erwin sisters asked her to make a demonstration tape of one of their newly written songs, since their current lead singer, Laura, was away on a trip with her daughter. But Natalie knew they were seriously considering her as a replacement for Laura when they started asking her how she felt about traveling with a band. Explaining the reasons behind their choice, Emily said, "We know we will always be playing music together, so we wanted to find someone who is just as determined and energetic as we are." Natalie fit that description exactly. She confesses she had always admired the band from afar, and said that "I loved watching them play. I didn't know what I was going to do. I just knew I wanted to sing." After many false starts, the once-confused student had found her chosen career path.

One evening Emily and Martie went to Laura's house to ask if they could buy out her share of the Dixie Chicks' corporation. Laura agreed to this, but she wanted the public to know that she had not quit the band. The Erwins informed Laura that Natalie was their first choice for a new

The Dixie Chicks, who were told by Natalie that she "wasn't going to wear those cowgirl clothes," discarded their previous look and adopted an edgier, more contemporary style.

lead singer. Bass player Bobby Charles Jr.—who had recently been permanently hired—and new guitarist Tom Nash were shocked to hear about Laura's departure from the group, even going to Laura's house to comfort her.

Emily admits the bond among the three women has grown since Natalie joined the group in 1995. "Natalie at this point is like a sister," she said. "We respect her as an artist, but we know her family, we know she came from a great foundation. . . . and was someone we could get along with as a friend as well as a bandmate." Perhaps the pesky age gap that had not affected the group's chemistry in the past had caught up with the Erwin sisters. The musical styles and life concerns of two women in their twenties were just not the same as those of Laura, who was a 37-year-old single mother.

Basically, the Chicks had to choose between remaining a group on the fringe of mainstream success or joining the larger country music community of Nashville. As Emily would put it, "We were really at the point where we were wanting that major-label success." However, the Chicks were not about to become a formulaic corporate country act. They would always maintain their inclusion of the old-time fiddle and steel guitar sounds in their music. Their bluegrass and traditional training were not going to disappear overnight; they would combine the best of their old style infused with some of the new sounds that their contemporaries such as Tim McGraw and Shania Twain were producing.

Natalie promptly left Texas Tech University, where she had been taking a course called Introductory Wildlife, and scrambled to learn 30 songs in three days in preparation for the upcoming Dixie Chicks tour. Her boyfriend and future husband, Michael, volunteered to drive the blue tour van. She was ready to hit the highways of America with the Dixie Chicks. Natalie, as much as she respected the past history of the Dixie Chicks, was not interested in joining a "frilly cowgirl" act. She put one condition to her new bandmates: "The only thing I knew for sure was that I wasn't going to wear those cowgirl clothes." The time for great change had come in the form of the petite blond, blue-eyed Texan. Martie would agree that a new era was starting for the chicks, with Natalie as the catalyst of change. "With Natalie," she said of the Chicks' evolution, "that's when the wheels started rolling around. You could tell there was excitement. There was energy."

5

CHICKS RULE!

The rise to stardom for the Dixie Chicks was brought about by many factors: the early marketing genius of Laura Lynch, their hard work ethic on the road, an overall dedication to quality musicianship, and the Internet. The Chicks were among the first musical groups to take advantage of the publicity opportunities provided by the information superhighway. Robert Wilonsky of the Dallas *New Times* wrote, "No band in town ever worked harder to get further; outsiders will write of their overnight success, but the Chicks know better."

One of the most notable early websites devoted entirely or in part to the Dixie Chicks was run by Dallas radio personality Katie Pruett. The most detailed early Dixie Chicks website belonged to Robert Brooks of Dallas. The website was Robert's hobby for several years. In March 1999, the Dixie Chicks' management bought the rights to the website name, *www.dixiechicks.com* from him. Robert now runs the website called *www.dixiechicks.mixedsignal.net*, which includes an unauthorized history of the Chicks, a complete timeline of their career, *Chick Chat* archives from the group's old newsletter, MP3 song sample files, and plenty of pictures.

With their images being viewed by millions of people on television, the Internet, and in live performances, it is not

The Dixie Chicks with one of their idols, Emmylou Harris. The Chicks were now starting to find success and in 1996 signed a major label recording contract.

surprising the girls have a huge following. Some of their male fans even send marriage proposals and pictures of themselves. As their careers began to dominate their time, it was difficult for the Dixie Chicks to maintain their personal lives. Martie did find time to fall in love with Ted Ashley Seidel, a pharmaceutical salesman who had a son, Carter, from his first marriage. Amidst Martie's growing fame, the couple set aside a wedding date of June 17, 1995. The traditional wedding was held at St. Luke's Episcopal Church in Dallas, and the upscale reception was held on the top floor at an undisclosed high-rise building. Unfortunately, both Martie's and Natalie's marriages did not survive fame and fortune. Natalie was divorced in November 1999. She and Michael Tarabay barely had any time together since their 1997 wedding. True to her character, Natalie was very vocal in public about seeking a divorce from Michael. Martie herself was divorced by early February 2000. The strains of life on the road with the band had not allowed her to properly "settle down" with her new husband and stepchild; the couple claimed they had "irreconcilable differences." Ted had even quit his job to be a househusband in an effort to be there for his family.

The cost of fame had been high for Martie and Natalie's personal lives. The last hope for love clung to Emily, who fell in love with country singer Charlie Robison early in 1998. The couple married at a ranch near Dallas on May 1, 1999. At the 1999 American County Music Awards, Natalie jokingly thanked Robison "because we never thought anyone would marry Emily."

The group's nationwide popularity took off with the release of *Wide Open Spaces*. This was their first album with Sony's Monument label. In

1996 the Chicks had visited the corporate head-quarters of Sony in Japan. (Always adventurous, they had found some time for snorkeling in rough Pacific waters.) The Monument label had chosen the Dixie Chicks to be their cornerstone act. The label had been barren of notable talent for quite some time, and it was looking to the group to revive it. The Dixie Chicks toured the United States coast to coast from August to December 1997 to publicize their first album with their new label.

Fame came with a price as Martie divorced in 2000, finding that life on the road had not helped her relationship with her husband and stepchild.

The first single released from *Wide Open Spaces* was "I Can Love You Better." In less than a month it was in heavy rotation on country radio, and by mid-November it was for sale at music stores. "Give It Up or Let Me Go," written by Bonnie Raitt, was soulfully interpreted by Natalie. The band's official statement about the album's title track included this statement: "We thought 'Wide Open Spaces,' written by West Texas songstress Susan Gibson, would be the title cut 'cause it's about going out there and chasing a dream." That song was *their* own story, and they were living out those lyrics.

> *Who doesn't know what I'm talking about*
> *Who's never left home, who's never struck out*
> *To find a dream and a life of their own*
> *A place in the clouds, a foundation of stone*
>
> *Many precede and many will follow*
> *A young girl's dream no longer hollow*
> *It takes the shape of a place out West*
> *But what it holds for her, she hasn't*
>   *yet guessed*
>
> Chorus:
> *She needs wide open spaces*
> *Room to make her big mistakes*
> *She needs new faces*
> *She knows the high stakes*

The Dixie Chicks took their share of chances over the years, sacrificing their time, effort, and personal relationships and for the success of the group. The *Wide Open Spaces* album would prove to the world that the Chicks could be included in the among the greatest stars of contemporary country music. Despite the high stakes posed by the fickle music industry, the Chicks had triumphed with this album!

By the end of 1998 the album sales would reach three million (categorized as "triple platinum" in the record industry). To date, *Wide Open Spaces* has sold over 11 million copies. The Chicks hold the record for highest-selling album by a group in the history of country music; the album is one of the Top 100 albums of all time, and it is the highest-selling debut album in the history of country music. Critical as well as popular praise was lavished on them as their debut album received two Country Music Association Awards, two Grammy Awards, three Academy of Country Music Awards, and an American Music Award. It's no wonder the president of Sony Nashville, Allen Butler, refers to the golden-haired trio as "the real deal."

Even people who usually are not interested in the country music genre were sitting up and taking notice of the Texan trio—and they liked what they heard. The follow-up to *Wide Open Spaces* was entitled *Fly* and was released in August 1999. *Wide Open Spaces* was a hard debut to follow,

Critics couldn't stop talking about the Dixie Chicks and audiences couldn't stop buying their albums, eventually setting a record for highest-selling debut album in the history of country music with *Wide Open Spaces*.

considering that album's colossal success. But *Fly* received rave reviews from the major American entertainment publications such as *Rolling Stone, Request, Entertainment Weekly,* and many others. Again, Allen Butler complimented the Dixie Chicks, writing, "They have an excellent sense of who they are musically and as an act overall, and they have grown tremendously as performers, musicians and especially as songwriters. . . . Their music is firmly rooted in country, but they're that rare act that knows no boundaries."

Unlike their first album with Monument, which contained only one original composition ("You Were Mine"), *Fly* contains more of their own original work. While writing the album, the Chicks often took retreats to unlock their creativity. When they were making the album, the members were either struggling with the end of a relationship (Natalie) or rejoicing at a new love (Emily). This is certainly reflected in angry songs such as "Hole in My Head" in which the singer insults her loser boyfriend, as opposed to the romantic "Cowboy Take Me Away," which has been sung at two of the three Dixie Chicks' wedding receptions. Martie told the Nashville *Tennessean* how influential real life was on the *Fly* album, admitting that "Emily's wedding and Natalie's divorce set the whole tone."

The well-known track "Ready to Run" was featured in the soundtrack for *Runaway Bride,* the 1999 film starring Julia Roberts and Richard Gere. The film's popularity helped the sales of *Fly*. The album went to number one on the *Billboard* 200 Chart and won the award for Best Country Album at the 2000 Grammy Awards as well as awards from Country Music Television, *Billboard* magazine, the Country Music Awards, the American Academy of Country Music, and the American Music Awards. As of July 2001, it had sold eight million copies.

The Dixie Chicks promoted their second album with yet another tour in 2000. The primarily young, female audience members were heard to be shouting the slogan, "Chicks Rule!" The Chicks also used their concerts as an opportunity to teach younger country fans about their own idols and friends, Willie Nelson and Ricky Scaggs, who joined them onstage at certain performances. Emily told *USA Weekend*, "Our music and what we do, touring and running our own company, hopefully inspired young girls to go out and do whatever *they* want to do."

6

CHICKS COURT CONTROVERSY

In addition to gaining new fans and pleasing their old ones, two of the songs on the *Fly* album sparked controversy due to their subjects and lyrics. In "Good-bye Earl" a woman who is abused by her husband murders him with the help of her good friend.

> *Well it wasn't two weeks*
> *After she got married that*
> *Wanda started getting abused*
> *She put on dark glasses and long sleeved blouses*
> *And make up to cover the bruise*
> *Well she finally got the nerve to file for divorce*
> *She let the law take it from there*
> *But Earl walked right through that restraining order*
> *And put her in intensive care*
> *Right away Mary Anne flew in from Atlanta*
> *On a red eye midnight flight*
> *She held Wanda's hand as they*
> *Worked out a plan*
> *And it didn't take 'em long to decide*
> *That Earl had to die*

The equally controversial video for the hit single starred high-profile actors. Dennis Franz, from *NYPD Blue*, plays the abusive

The Dixie Chicks perform "Sin Wagon," one of the songs that have aroused some controversy among critics.

husband; Jane Krakowski, of *Ally McBeal*, is the long-suffering wife; and her helpful friend is played by actress Lauren Holly. This was not the first time—and nor will it probably be the last—that the Dixie Chicks find their artistic morals questioned. After releasing the song and accompanying video, the group wanted to convey the fact that they don't recommend violence for solving personal disputes, making the disclaimer that "[The] Dixie Chicks do not advocate premeditated violence, but love getting even." On a positive note, the National Coalition Against Domestic Violence supported the song for bringing needed attention to this societal problem.

Another song from *Fly* that caught the attention of critics is "Sin Wagon." The song, co-written by Natalie and Emily, is about a girl letting loose and sowing her wild oats after she has been a "good girl" for her entire life. Natalie describes the song as the story of a girl "who's been good for way too long and goes out and does all her sinning in one night." (Originally, the women wanted to call the *Fly* album *Sin Wagon*; however, the record executives feared that the title would not cast a good light on the spunky good-girl image of the group.) Maybe the record executives were worried, but the fans loved this song and identified with the message. Though the girl "sins" in one verse, in the next verse she asks God's forgiveness:

> *When it's my turn to march up to glory*
> *I'm gonna have one hell of a story*
> *That's if He forgives me*
> *Oh Lord Please forgive me*
> *Praise the Lord and pass the ammunition*
> *Need a little bit more of that sweet salvation*
> *They may take me*
> *With my feet draggin'*
> *But I'll fly away on a sin wagon*

There are also remarks in the song made about ammunition. The United States had recently been jolted by outbreaks of student violence, most horribly at Columbine High School in Columbine, Colorado. "Sin Wagon" hit a raw nerve with advocates of stricter gun control laws. Due to the song's edgy content, Sony Monument chose not release the single first. But the Dixie Chicks stood by their work and both songs had to remain on the album.

Another fact about the Dixie Chicks that has brought them some negative press coverage has been their fashion sense, which has been called "trashy." Natalie has been compared with Madonna in her performances (more for her shocking almost punk or new-wave look than for being too outlandishly sexy). Parents are always concerned that young girls, especially preteens, receive the wrong message from female performers. This is most obvious in their concern about the outfits worn by pop idols Britney Spears and Christina Aguillera. But the Dixie Chicks don't want to be typecast. On the contrary, they want the music to speak for itself—which is why they refuse to shy away from thought-provoking subject matter in their songs. Natalie doesn't hesitate to proclaim, "Were doing what we want to do. We're playing what we want to play. We're looking like we want to look. We're saying what we want to say. In other genres, that's OK but in country, the attitude tends to be more 'I'm just happy to be here.'"

The Dixie Chicks didn't set out to be provocative in some planned way, they're just growing up and taking their fans along for the ride as they explore and examine important issues in their own lives. In their early days, the Dixie Chicks were on the brink of becoming a novelty act by staying with their western cowgirl outfits and mostly bluegrass sound. Emily began to fear that people weren't listening to the music and that "people were starting to come to shows to see what we were wearing." That was not at all what they were working toward with their music. They weren't just pretty young girls. They were country artists. Martie explains how they used this traditional clothing as a gimmick, saying "We knew it was a little different. But we grew to the point where we really wanted the music to speak for itself." They feel that they have the right to speak their minds because they have the talent and life experiences to back it all up.

When compared with the big-haired, all-American, conservative yet glamorous look of past country stars such as Barbara Mandrell, the distinct look of the Dixie Chicks does have some shock value. The women admit that they are not the first to shock country audiences. And they point out Shania Twain as a pioneer in the new look of country music. As Natalie puts it, "Shania Twain was the first Shania Twain and anybody who's tried to follow isn't quite Shania Twain . . . "

Even before the release of *Wide Open Spaces*, the Dixie Chicks saw that their influence was reaching beyond their core market of female teenage fans. When they opened for the George Strait tour, the older, more traditional country fans—though a little disoriented by their unorthodox stage show at first—were soon dancing right alongside the teenagers. The enthusiasm for the group was contagious.

It's not only about the cosmetics, the hair, or the flashy clothes. The Dixie Chicks are an *attitude*. When they tie feather boas to their microphone

stands, they are not just advertising sexiness, they are celebrating their right to be women. The Dixie Chicks are aware that they are living at a time when female musicians of all musical styles are taking over the airwaves. The late 1990s saw the rise of a whole new breed of female performer such as Gwen Stefani (of the pop-rock band No Doubt), Lauryn Hill (formerly of the Fugees), singer-songwriter Jewel, and others who were redefining musical tastes and dominating record sales. Emily knew that the group could be part of this particular historical moment when she said,

The Dixie Chicks won a Grammy for "There's Your Trouble." The girls were being recognized by the recording industry for their achievements and saw their appeal expand beyond country music's borders.

"Right now, it's a great time for many of us because there have been so many women who have opened the doors. The women are selling the albums right now, which is what is so cool. It's not just that the music is great, they're actually selling the product." Perhaps audiences were tired of men and their opinions and tastes dominating the charts for so many years. Female recording artists of all musical styles could join in the fun (as well as the controversies) and the action that the men had been involved in for years.

In the United States, which prides itself on freedom of expression and freedom for men and women to speak their minds, nothing could be more American than the Dixie Chicks and their battle cries for equality between men and women. The women took this feeling of empowerment to the stage in the summer of 1999 when they performed at the Lilith Fair. The fair was started in July 1997 by Canadian singer-songwriter Sarah McLachlan. It is a tour that showcases an all-female lineup of groups and performers. The Dixie Chicks received complaints from the Religious Right that they were once again selling out to the devil. The *National Liberty Journal* in particular made a connection between the festival's name and "the demonic legend of the mystical woman whose name the series manifests."

The female performers at the Lilith Fair have been associated with a radical branch of the feminist movement. Even mainstream magazines such as *Entertainment Weekly* mocked the festival. As country singers, the Dixie Chicks were representing their chosen form of self-expression—country music. They were asked to be one of the tour's co-headliners, along with R&B star Monica and the legendary group the Pretenders (led by Chrissie Hynde). The Chicks were undaunted by the negative press. They wore capri pants in hot pink and army green along with their usual heavily-applied makeup and glitter. They wouldn't change their look. They play the style game on their own terms. The Dixie Chicks continue to voice their feminist spirit. Martie told *Seventeen* magazine, "Women don't need to be so defensive anymore. First work hard, do what you do best, and reap the rewards."

7

CHICKS IN
THE NEW MILLENIUM

So far the new century has been good to the Dixie Chicks—both personally and professionally—albeit at a little slower pace than the late 1990s. From 1999 through 2000, the group was touring constantly all over the United States. In the summer of 1999 they also made some changes in their band. Both guitarist Tommy Nash and bass player Bobby Charles Jr. were replaced before the new millenium began.

Natalie married actor Adrian Pasdar on June 24, 2001, at the Little White Wedding Chapel on the Las Vegas Strip. The couple met when they were both in Emily and Charlie's wedding party. Adrian, who is an old friend of Charlie's, is an actor who was living in Los Angeles when he met his future wife. He is 10 years older than Natalie and has a sophisticated sense of humor to match her wit. Since Adrian was unable to attend the 2000 Academy of Country Music Awards, he gave Natalie a bulldog puppy named Ralph to take his place. Ralph is now the group's unofficial mascot.

Adrian currently stars in the television series *Mysterious Ways*, which airs on the PAX television network. He portrays an anthropology professor named Declan Dunn. He has also acted in many films and directed short films including music videos for Paula Abdul and his friend Charlie Robison.

The Dixie Chicks have found tremendous professional success in the past few years, but they've also found personal success with new loves in their lives.

In August 2000, Adrian was a guest on the popular *Live With Regis* program. He announced that Natalie was expecting the couple's first child. Natalie gave birth to her first child, Jackson Slade, on March 15, 2001. "Jack," as he is called, was born at about 10 A.M. at the Seton Medical Center in Austin, Texas and weighed in at 6 lbs., 20 oz. "Uncle" Charlie Robison announced the happy arrival on national television at Austin's Waterloo Park. He dedicated a performance of "The Wedding Song," which he had recorded as a duet with Natalie, to Natalie's new joy as Emily and Martie sat in the audience.

In October 2000, the Chicks decided to slow down a bit in 2001 and take a break from the spotlight. As far as the Dixie Chicks are concerned, Natalie sees a bright future for the group. "I have a feeling that if we're around for 20 years," she says, "there will still be things we do that scare them."

Martie is happy to be at such a great place in her career with the Dixie Chicks. As the eldest member of the group, Martie finds it difficult to keep her emotions in check at times. "Sometimes," she admits, "I get onstage and get all choked up—seriously!" Since 1999 she has successfully moved on from her divorce from Ted Seidel. During her acceptance speech at the 1999 Grammy Awards, she even sent Ted and his son a special message: "I will always love you." With wisdom beyond her 32 years, Martie says, "I feel like now is the good old days. I think right now is the proving stage, to prove that we're for real." Martie wants to cement the group's place in the world of country, though she knows that stars rise and fall quickly in the entertainment business. "There's no guarantee that won't happen to us," she says. But fans can be sure Martie will work as hard as possible to keep

their audience happy and singing along.

Emily and Charlie Robison continue to strive for a more perfect life. They purchased a home in Bandera, Texas in 1999 that was close to Charlie's parents. It has not been easy for Charlie to adjust to being "Mr. Emily Erwin." In 1999 one country music reviewer wrote, "Charlie Robison's *Lucky Day* debut album arrives at a time when many people are apt to say 'Oh yeah. He's guy who's getting married to Emily Erwin of the Dixie Chicks.'" But Charlie also paid his dues in the Texas music scene as a songwriter and deserves respect for his efforts.

Emily's husband Charlie Robison is a country artist as well who has had to shrug off the title "Mr. Emily Erwin" in his own career.

At the 2000 Academy of Country Music Awards, Emily had dark hair, which really set her apart from her blond bandmates. She has often been cast as the introverted, quiet member of the Chicks, but Natalie thinks this is far from the truth: "[A] lot of people think Emily is the nice, shy one. . . . She's stranger than any of us!"

After the Lilith Fair experience, the Dixie Chicks were asked if they ever consider changing musical genre to pop or rock. Natalie replied, "No. We have no plans to ask any other radio format to play our records. Country music is our heritage, it's what we are, and what we will continue to be." Trying to broaden their audience didn't necessarily mean they were trying to break away from country music and all it has given to their lives.

In 2000 the Dixie Chicks won over a dozen different awards for *Fly*, and in 2001 they won the TNN/Country Music Television Award for Favorite Group or Duo. There is no doubt that they will continue to collect various awards and have more chick feet tattooed on the tops of their feet for years to come.

The Dixie Chicks show the value and strength of determination, hard work, pride in that work, and family togetherness. They have pride in their work, but try to stay grounded. Natalie explains, "We're confident in our music and sound, but not in a cocky way. But if you're not confident in your music, then who else will be?" Whether they are spending quality time with their loved ones or writing more chart-topping hits, they are going to do these things with that same Dixie Chick spirit, that same can-do attitude, and the same joy that they transmit to their fans.

In 11 years, the Dixie Chicks went from a cowgirl quartet with lots of spunk to an electrifying trio breaking all the rules. They have much to be proud of and much to be thankful for. They communicate that feeling of excitement to their audience whenever they pick up their instruments and microphones. Maybe it's because they never lost sight of the journey they are on. As Martie points out, "It's that way of doing things that I think has gotten us where we are. It made us stick with it. It's an adventure."

CHRONOLOGY

1969   Martha Eleanor ("Martie") Erwin is born on October 12 in York, Pennsylvania.

1972   Emily Erwin is born on August 16 in Pittsfield, Massachusetts.

1974   Natalie Maines is born on October 14 in Lubbock, Texas.

1989   Emily and Martie meet Laura Lynch and Robin Macy. They form a band and perform on street corners in Dallas. The band names itself the Dixie Chicks, after Little Feat's song, "Dixie Chicken."

1990   Debut album, *Thank Heavens for Dale Evans*, is released. They are booked to open for Garth Brooks, Emmylou Harris, Reba McIntyre, and George Strait.

1991   Debut performance at the Grand Ole Opry.

1992   Robin Macy leaves the band and guitarist Matt Benjamin replaces her. *Little Ol' Cowgirl* is released.

1993   Release of third independent CD, *Shouldn't a Told You That*. Perform at the 1993 Inaugural Ball of President Bill Clinton.

1995   Sign record contract with Sony Records on June 16. The group performs with country legend Loretta Lynn. Natalie joins the group. Martie and Emily buy out Laura's share of the band. Perform at Inaugural Gala for Governor George W. Bush of Texas.

1996   Signed by the Monument imprint of Sony records.

1998   *Wide Open Spaces* is released; "I Can Love You Better" becomes the band's first Top Ten single. Group wins the Horizon Award and Best Group at the CMAs.

1999   Receive American Music Awards, Grammy Awards, Academy of Country Music Awards, TNN Music City News Country Awards, and Country Music Association Awards. On August 31, *Fly* is released and reaches number one on the country charts.

2000   Embark on their *Fly* tour from June to December.

2001   The group performs in the fundraiser event, "America: A
            Tribute to Heroes," to raise money for the families of those
            who died in the terrorist attacks on New York and
            Washington, D.C. on September 11, 2001.

Accomplishments

Singles

1991   "Home on the Radar Range"

1998   "I Can Love You Better"
"There's Your Trouble"
"Wide Open Spaces"
"You Were Mine"

1999   "Cowboy Take Me Away"

2000   "Good-bye Earl"

Albums

1991   *Thank Heavens for Dale Evans*

1992   *Little Ol' Cowgirl*

1993   *Shouldn't a Told You That*

1998   *Wide Open Spaces*

1999   *Fly*

Awards

1991   *Dallas Observer* Best Country and Western Band of the Year

1998   *Billboard* Award   Best New Country Artist Clip of the Year— "Wide Open Spaces," Maximum Vision Clip of the Year— "Wide Open Spaces"

Country Music Association Horizon Award and Group of the Year

Country Music Television Awards Rising Star

Grammy Awards Best Country Album—*Wide Open Spaces*, Best Country Vocal Performance Duo/Group—"There's Your Trouble"

National Association of Record Merchandisers Best Selling Artist by a New Artist/Group—"Wide Open Spaces"

Pollstar's Concert Industry Award Best New Artist Tour

Roughstock Best New Artist

1999   Academy of Country Music Awards

Album of the Year—*Wide Open Spaces*, Top New Vocal Duet or Group, and Top Duet or Group

American Music Awards Favorite New Country Artist

Billboard Awards Country Artist of the Year, Country Group/Duo, Country Album Artist of the Year, Best New Country Artist Clip of the Year—"Ready to Run"

British Country Music Award International Rising Star

Canadian Country Music Award Best Selling Album—*Wide Open Spaces*

Country Music Television Awards Top Video "Ready to Run"

Country Music Association Best Music Video of the Year— "Wide Open Spaces," Group of the Year, Single of the Year—"Wide Open Spaces"

Country Weekly Golden Pick Favorite New Group/Duo

Grammy Awards Best Performance by a Country Duo or Group—"There's Your Trouble" and Best Country Album—*Fly*

TNN Music City News Country Awards Female Star of Tomorrow and Vocal Band of the Year

WB Radio Music Awards Country Artist of the Year, Country Song of the Year—"Wide Open Spaces"

2000 American Country Music Awards Album of the Year—*Fly* and Vocal Duo/Group of the Year

Billboard Award Country Artist of the Year, Country Album Artist of the Year, Country Artist Duo/Group of the Year, Album of the Year—*Fly*.

Blockbuster Music Award Favorite Country Duo/Group

British Country Music Award International Album—*Fly* and International Group/Duo

Canadian Country Music Award Best Selling Album—*Fly*

Country Music Association Album of the Year—*Fly*, Entertainer of the Year, Video of the Year—"Goodbye Earl," Vocal Group of the Year.

Country Music Television Group of the Year

Entertainment Weekly's Best of the Breed

Grammy Awards Best Country Album—*Fly*, and Best Performance by a Country Duo or Group—"Ready to Run"

Radio Music Awards Country Song of the Year—"Cowboy Take Me Away"

TNN/CW Awards Vocal Duo/Group, Album—*Fly*

2001 American Country Music Awards Entertainer of the Year, Vocal Group of the Year, Video of the Year—"Goodbye Earl"

American Music Awards Best Country Group or Duo

TNN/CW Favorite Group or Duo

Accolades

1998	*Entertainment Weekly*'s Breakout Acts of 1998
	Rolling Stone's Essential Records
	One of *People* magazine's 25 Most Intriguing People as Breakthrough Act
	Billboard's Top New Country Artist
	Country Monitor's Most Significant New Country Act
1999	*Billboard*'s Top Country Artist
	Rolling Stone's Country Artist of the Year
	One of *Entertainment Weekly*'s Entertainers of the Year
	Us magazine's "99 Stories of 1999"
2000	*Us* magazine's 6th "Most Unforgettable Story of 2000" for "Goodbye Earl"

FURTHER READING

Dickerson, James L. *Women on Top: The Quiet Revolution That's Rocking the American Music Industry*. New York: Billboard Books, 1998.

Emery, Ralph. *50 Years Down a Country Road*. New York: HarperCollins, 2000.

Moses, Robert, Alicia Potter, and Beth Rowen. *A&E Entertainment Almanac*. Boston and New York: Houghton Mifflin Co., 1996.

Oermann, Robert K., and Mary A. Burwack. *Finding Her Voice: The Saga of Women in Country Music*. New York: Crown Publishers, 1993.

ABOUT THE AUTHOR

CONCETTA SEMINARA-KENNEDY is a freelance writer, editor, and translator. She earned an M.A. in English and Publishing from Rosemont College (1999). Concetta lives in Far Hills, New Jersey, with her husband.

INDEX